THE LITTLE GUIDE
GUIDE
to Palmistry

HOW TO READ ANYONE'S UNIQUE
PERSONALITY AND POTENTIAL
FROM THEIR HANDS

THE LITTLE
GUIDE
to Palmistry

JOHNNY FINCHAM

WATKINS
1893

The Little Guide to Palmistry
Johnny Fincham

First published as *Palmistry at Your Fingertips*
in the UK and USA in 2013 by Watkins,
an imprint of Watkins Media Limited

This edition published in 2023 by
Watkins, an imprint of Watkins Media Limited
Unit 11, Shepperton House, 83–93 Shepperton Road
London N1 3DF

enquiries@watkinspublishing.com

Commissioning Editor: Ella Chappell
Copyeditor: Brittany Willis
Head of Design: Karen Smith
Designer: Steve Williamson
Illustrator: Sneha Alexander
Production: Uzma Taj

A CIP record for this book is available from the British Library

ISBN: 978-1-78678-776-7 (Hardback)
ISBN: 978-1-78678-777-4 (eBook)

10 9 8 7 6 5 4 3 2 1

Printed in the United Kingdom by TJ Books Ltd

www.watkinspublishing.com

MIX
Paper from
responsible sources
FSC   FSC® C013056

CONTENTS

INTRODUCTION

Palmistry was traditionally a form of divination, focusing exclusively on the palm lines. From these lines, people would make fatalistic predictions of love, of life, of death, of good and bad fortune. We placed great importance on special line markings such as the "star of fortune" or the "sacred triangle". As a result, hand reading often incurs a heavy burden of fear, superstition and scepticism.

It's the broader aspects of palmistry — the relative length of the digits, the fingerprint patterns, the shape of the palm, the skin texture — that science has verified as accurate indications of a person's character. Early psychologists, such as Julius Spier, Karl Jung and Charlotte Wolfe, established concrete links between palm features, intelligence and personality, moving the art of palmistry away from the mystical and into the realm of science. In very recent times, anthropological researchers have conducted experiments proving that if certain fingers are particularly large or small, these reflect distinct personality traits. As such, palmistry has moved beyond looking at only line markings on your palm.

Palmistry has never been more powerful, progressive and vibrant than now. In medical research, psychology, anthropology and genetics, the palm is proving to be an incredible mirror into the inner workings of the mind. The brain area allocated to the hands is larger than that focused on any other part of the body, using a vast part of the cerebrum in terms of motor and neural connections. Its relative size in terms of brain area would make your hands the size of house doors!

As we begin this book, we must first understand palmistry not just as a fatalistic, determining art, but most importantly as a mirror for self-understanding. While the palm indicates the overall fixed characteristics of a subject, the lines of the palm change over time, so no pattern marked on the palm is fixed. Our lives are literally and figuratively in our own hands.

A BRIEF HISTORY OF PALMISTRY

Humans have always been fascinated by their hands. If we take a deep dive into history, even prehistoric cave dwellers saw their hands as markers of their individuality. Anthropologists argue that the palm prints found in prehistoric caves around the world were our ancestors' attempts to leave a personal signature of ownership. As each palm print is unique, this would have shown exactly who lived in which cave.

The study of palmistry has made its way around the globe throughout the years. The first documented practice of palm reading we have is from India: *The Teachings of Valmiki*

Maharshi on Male Palmistry was written around 2000 BC with its roots in Hindu astrology. From there, it made its way to China, Sumeria, Persia, Egypt and Greece. Many renowned historical figures studied palmistry, including Aristotle, Hippocrates and Alexander the Great.

Palmistry has always been kept in the shadows to some extent, being forbidden by all the major religions, including the Catholic Church (even though palmistry is mentioned in the bible three times!). It only thrived when the power of monolithic religious structures declined. For example, during the Reformation in England, interest in palmistry and astrology flourished. Thomas Cromwell mentioned in his journal that he'd had his hand read in Italy and was prophesized to achieve greatness. There are also numerous examples of people turning to palmistry during the Weimar Republic in Germany – even Albert Einstein had his palms read.

Easily the most popular palm reader in history was the great Cheiro (1866–1936) who achieved worldwide celebrity status in his time, reading for such notables as Oscar Wilde, Mark Twain, General Kitchener, Thomas Edison and the Prince of Wales.

In recent times, palm reading has emerged into popular culture as fascination with alternative spirituality has blossomed. Science and medical research have also examined the palm and established that markings, finger difference and prints on the hands manifest in individual characteristics.

WHAT HAND READING CAN AND CAN'T TELL YOU

Palmistry is principally a means of self-knowledge. It isn't a form of fortune telling. No tall, dark, handsome strangers are marked in your hand, nor will it tell you how long you'll live. However, truly astonishing information can be gleaned from the palm: sensitivity, emotional balance, confidence, intelligence and numerous other qualities.

The lines on the palm change as time goes on, reflecting new patterns of behaviour. Due to how quickly children's hands change, changes in the palm lines of children are particularly obvious and easy to see. As you grow older, fingers bend, lines get longer or shorter and markings appear and vanish. Always bear in mind that the markings you see now may be different in a year's time. If you take prints of your palms (see page 14) at regular intervals, you'll be able to clearly track the changes that occur to your palms as time goes by.

HOW TO GET THE MOST FROM THIS BOOK

Each chapter offers a plethora of information, so make sure you can fully grasp the concepts of one before you move onto the next. I have included learning points at the end of each chapter to help you absorb the information.

It might also be helpful to look at real-life examples. Your own palms are easily accessible to you and can be a great resource as you learn, but I recommend you also ask your friends and family to offer their palms up for your lessons. This will allow you to compare different markings and different examples. After all, every palm is different. For example, when you learn what a whorl fingerprint means and what it looks like (see page 49), try to find a whorl on the finger of someone you know. Talk to them about how they experience the characteristics associated with a whorl print. It's important to get comfortable looking at hands as soon as you can, using this book as a guide. All beginner palmists feel they don't know enough to start reading hands but as you acquire experience and learn how true and powerful the process is, your confidence and ability will soar.

One essential point to bear in mind in any reading is: **ignore anything common or average**. You're always looking for points that make someone unique; any feature considered common, like an average finger length or a common ulnar loop print (see page 48) can be happily ignored. This will make your job as a reader much easier.

A palm reading is a balancing act. Never take a single marking and see this as a character trait on its own. You must also consider the shape of the palm, the skin texture, the fingers and other factors. Every element is only one piece of the puzzle in a larger picture. The skill of a good palmist lies in the ability to put observations together and formulate a balanced picture of an individual.

Don't take my word for it – check everything for yourself. If you learn that people with coarse skin are outdoors types, go out and find a farmer or fisherman and see what kind of skin they have. You need to own the secret language of palmistry and prove its worth for yourself.

LEARNING POINTS

Palmistry is about self-understanding, not predictions

Palm lines aren't fixed; they change as we grow and adopt new characteristics

Read the whole hand, not just a single marking

Use what you learn in real life by looking at the palms (and fingers) of your friends, family, coworkers, etc

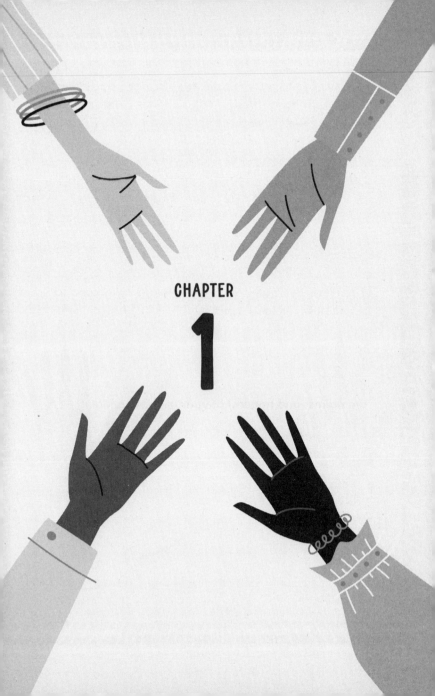

CHAPTER

1

GETTING TO KNOW THE HAND

When you first look at someone's hands, it's difficult to know where to begin. A palm reading is about translating your observations and impressions into clear, understandable character traits and personal qualities. Try not to rush, and weigh up each point carefully. It's important to work through the palm systematically, stage by stage, chapter by chapter, as you work through this book.

FIRST IMPRESSIONS

The first impression is always important – never discount it. Don't worry if this doesn't come naturally to you at first. Practice makes perfect, and you'll learn what to watch out for. I've included some of my top tips for what to focus on below. Have a look at your own hands, or the hands of a close friend, and see what your first impressions are using this guidance.

However, be wary of fully trusting your first impression and not looking further. As a hand reader, you must learn to trust what the palm is telling you, not what traits your client is displaying. For example, the palms of a raving, loud extrovert may show signs of tremendous insecurity and lack of confidence. You must learn to trust the truth of what the palm is revealing to you, not the surface personality.

So, use the below guidance to make your first impressions, then come back to your initial thoughts after you have taken a full reading of the same hand. How did you do?

HAND SIZE

First, how big is the palm of the person you're reading? In most cases, the size of the hand is roughly in proportion to the size of the person. But occasionally, a palm is particularly large or small — as if it belongs to someone bigger or smaller than the person in question. Disproportionately large-handed people are good with details and enjoy working through everything meticulously. Dental technicians, surgeons, classical guitarists and jewellers usually have large hands. Those with small hands are the opposite: they work fast and tackle life head on. They seem to run at a higher speed than most people and are great at handling large projects as they can see the bigger picture, but they have little patience and no time for details. Small hands are found on sportspeople, those that perform in public and people who run fast-moving businesses.

ACTIVE AND PASSIVE HANDS

The hand we write and catch a ball with is our dominant or active palm. The dominant palm reveals our developed, outer, mature personality — the face we reveal to the world. The non-dominant or passive palm shows our subliminal, latent, inner personality. Often it reveals issues and drives that we're unaware of and that are part of our formative experiences. The passive hand is much more representative of how a person was in childhood. Only our parents and those intimate with us would know us as the person presented in the passive hand.

Both hands should be considered in a reading. The greater the difference between the palms, the more a person will develop and change through life. If the person is older, the active hand will likely express more of their personality, and more emphasis should be given to that hand. This is because they will have already lived a lot of their life and developed into the person they are. However, the passive hand still shows a hidden side of them that the world doesn't see, and so should not be fully discounted.

SPAN

Check the span by measuring across the palm, starting halfway up, just above the thumb. Now compare it with the length, which should be measured from just below the middle finger to the base of the palm. Is the palm broad, perhaps as wide as it is long? Or is it narrow, giving the hand a distinctly oblong shape? Broad palms show a fixed, stable, practical outlook. The person tends to seek order and to impose stability. If the palm is narrow, this indicates a more intuitive, instinctive and creative approach to life. Individuals with oblong-shaped palms are highly responsive to their environment and are strongly affected by other people. Those with very narrow palms can sometimes be psychologically sensitive and tend to be more introverted.

COLOUR

Colour can also indicate the person's character. Reddish, ruddy hands signify internal heat, repressed energy and passion. Pale, clammy palms show a lethargic disposition and a more passive attitude to life.

SKIN TEXTURE

The skin on the inside of the palm indicates the physical sensitivity of a person and how they react to the world around them. Skin texture can reveal a great deal about a person, including their diet, career, lifestyle and the type of relationship they want to have. The skin on the inner palm (and also on the soles of the feet) is covered with fine ridges and multiple sweat glands and nerve receptors. The coarser and rougher these ridges are, the more insensitive and tougher the personality. This is because the inner palm's surface indicates the complexity of a person's central nervous system.

There are two ways to measure the skin texture: you can simply feel the surface using the tip of your index finger, stroking it across the middle of the palm (or an area near the centre where there are no calluses); or you can look at the print of a hand (see pages 14–15) and examine the skin ridges and the number, density and quality of the lines present in detail.

THE FOUR PALM SKIN TYPES

There are four basic skin textures you will find on a person's palm, and each indicate a different thing.

SILK SKIN

If the skin feels ultra-fine and soft, or the print shows barely visible ridges and lots of fine lines, the person is hypersensitive – they have an aversion to conflict and harsh situations, and they are physically delicate with a fussy, fragile disposition. This skin type – known as silk skin – is common among alternative therapists, carers, spiritual seekers, intuitives, artists and aesthetes.

PAPER SKIN

If the skin feels papery, dry and is slightly yellow in colour, or the print shows tightly grained, fine skin ridges with long, scratchy lines, the person is cerebral, aware and highly visual. They are sensitive but a little cool on the surface, and responsive to ideas, images, speech, books, words and language. This skin type – known as paper skin – is common among teachers, office workers, call-centre operatives and anyone who uses technology and communication skills at work.

GRAINY SKIN

If the skin feels grainy, or the print shows firm, hard skin ridges with strong, red lines like cuts, the person is action-orientated. They are always busy and are by nature "doers". This skin type — known as grainy skin — is common among sporty and business-minded people. Grainy skin is much more common on males than on females.

COARSE SKIN

If the skin feels hard and rough, with ridges that look and feel like wood, or the print shows only a few deep lines, the person is a hardy, outdoors type. They are physically tough, manually skilled and more practical than emotional. This skin type — called coarse skin — is common among tree surgeons, farmers, fishermen, gardeners and manual workers. They are impervious to the outside temperature and love to keep moving. It's very rare to see coarse skin on a female, even if they work in farming, fishing or gardening.

MAKING HAND PRINTS

To examine a hand properly, and to record changes in the palms over time, you need to take prints. This is a skill that requires practice.

YOU WILL NEED:

- ★ black or brown block-printing, water-based ink

- ★ an ink roller

- ★ plain A4/US letter photocopying paper

- ★ a magnifying glass (optional, depending on your eyesight)

METHOD:

1. Work on a flat, smooth surface such as a table with a little padding – maybe a magazine – beneath the paper you're going to print onto.

2. Squeeze 1cm (½in) of ink onto any smooth, non-absorbent surface.

3. Roll the ink roller up and down in the ink until the roller is covered, but try to use the minimum possible.

4. Ask the person whose hands you're going to print to relax their hands. Working on one hand at a time, carefully roll the ink over the inner palm, covering the whole surface, including the fingers, with an even, thin layer. Follow the contours of the hand and dab the roller onto any bare patches.

5. Quickly press the palm onto the paper, using plenty of pressure on the fingers as well as the palm. If the palm has a large hollow in the centre, making it hard to obtain a print, lift the hand, and push the paper into the hollow.

6. Peel the paper away carefully and examine the print.

HAND SHAPE

In the early 1960s the palmist, artist and astrologer Fred Gettings revived a centuries-old method of categorizing palms that is extremely effective. He developed a fourfold system, dividing palms into the traditional elements of earth, water, fire and air. This works very well for the 70 per cent of people who have a clearly defined palm shape element. Unfortunately, 30 per cent of palms are undefined and difficult to categorize in this way. It's important to note that those who show a clear element always have some contradictions at a deeper level of analysis, which stop them conforming 100 per cent to any one element. However, when a hand does fall into a classic elemental pattern, it's a wonderful, powerful way of reading the overall nature of their character before you get into a detailed analysis. The elemental system takes the whole hand, including the fingers, into account. For this reason, I suggest you try and identify if your hands fit into any of the elemental categories now that you've had a good look at them, but then come back and try again once you've read Chapter 2 on getting to know your fingers.

EARTH HAND

Earth hands are square, thick and heavy. The hand is fleshy and well padded, there are very few lines and the fingers are short and stiff. Earth-handed people are usually short and thickset and have natural strength and endurance. They are endowed with practical, manual skills and are likely to have a craft, such as gardening, building or basketmaking. Their life view tends toward pragmatism, and they are sceptical of abstract philosophies, ideals and high-minded views. They trust only what's familiar and tried-and-tested. Family and home, tradition and the past are enormously important in earth consciousness. People with this hand type usually have large families, and, because they are reliable, unpretentious and stable, they make good parents. Often they will sacrifice opportunity in favour of security, and change is viewed with apprehension. Earth hands are displayed by those who do the crucial work that supports society, but that often goes unnoticed and unrewarded: care workers, cleaners, factory workers, lorry drivers, builders, sewage workers, farmers, gardeners and miners.

WATER HAND

Water hands have a narrow, rectangular palm. The fingers are long and flexible, and the lines are numerous, fine and delicate. Water types usually have pale skin and highly flexible joints. Often their eyes are expressive and their hair is worn long. The narrow nature of the palm makes a water person highly receptive to their environment. The water hand is a sign of a responsive, changeable nature, driven by impulse, sensation and emotion. Relationships dominate water people's consciousness. These individuals are also astute at making connections intuitively and creatively between ideas, objects and people. This gives them an intensely spiritual perspective, which often manifests in artistic qualities. Since they are driven by deeper impulses, water people tend to seek careers that are neither monotonous nor too physically demanding, such as alternative therapists, counsellors, religious professionals, artists, poets, social workers, those who work with children, life coaches, charity workers and beauticians. Water-handed people dislike disagreements and abhor competition. Instead, they tend to seek harmony and inner calm; hence relationships are prioritized over the pursuit of wealth or power. Goals are achieved by teamwork, through friendships and by cooperation with others.

FIRE HAND

Fire hands also have rectangular palms but they are not as narrow as water hands. The fingers are short (but not as short as earth fingers), the palm is warm and dry and the lines are deep and red. People with fire hands tend to have muscular or wiry physiques, short hair and intense eyes. They often find it difficult to relax, and usually try to switch off by playing sport or exercising. Fire-handed people are responsive, like those with water hands, but since they are broader with shorter fingers, consciousness is inclined toward change and action. Fire brings about transformation and heat, and people with fire hands are always interested in self-development, acquiring skills, moving on, going places and doing things. Fire naturally abhors water, so deeper feelings and emotions tend to be ignored, repressed or displaced. Career is crucial because these individuals often feel that what they do is what they are. Achievement, kudos and power are the means by which they seek fulfilment. They're best suited to work that is challenging and allows them to use their initiative: self-employment, management, entrepreneurial enterprises, the media, money markets, motivating other people – in fact, any situation that is fast-moving and has an element of excitement.

AIR HAND

Air hands have a square palm, but whereas the earth palm is thick-boned, the air palm has light, bird-like bones and the fingers are long. Air palms are the largest of the elemental hands and the palm is usually covered with lots of lines. The air-handed physique tends to be tall and thin. Often the person has visual problems, and their hair is extremely fine. They are the most prone to nervous and psychological stress, and the ability to be spontaneous and passionate is compromised by an ever-alert, ever-watchful mind. People with air hands are primarily conceptual in nature and tend toward thought, analysis and ideas. They can also veer toward non-conformism since they follow their own views on life. Journalists, writers, social commentators and comedians all tend to have such hands. The worlds of the university campus, of teaching, planning, consultancy, research and science are all air-hand dominated ones. Air is the principle of space, so air types like to work alone and to have a high degree of autonomy.

NO ELEMENTAL SHAPE

No clear hand shape? Don't worry if the hand doesn't conform to any of the elemental patterns. Some people have hands that are a mixture of elements. Some have hands that have a wedge shape, or a large bulge at the side so it's difficult to judge. When this is the case, simply ignore the shape and go onto the next level of analysis.

AREAS OF THE PALM

The palm is split in half from the centre of the middle finger down to the base of the palm. The side with the thumb and index finger is called the radial and the side with the ring finger and little finger is called the ulnar.

Knowing the difference between the radial and ulnar areas is important, as it helps you to understand why various lines and mounts mean what they do. The radial side reflects the conscious, tangible, physical world. All the mounts, markings and lines in this area are about ideas and realizations relating to family, home, the physical body, career, aspirations, personal power, ownership and influence. The ulnar side connects the unconscious, ephemeral aspects of life. This area reflects things that are less tangible: the outer world, other people,

Ulnar side

Radial side

travel to unknown regions, the depths of dreams and inner knowing, the social world and the drive to connect, explore, communicate and create.

THE PALM MOUNTS

The palm mounts – fleshy bumps on your palm – are situated just beneath each finger and around the circumference of the palm. Named after the moon and the planets and ascribed qualities associated with these heavenly bodies, the mounts were of paramount importance in the earliest palmistry books but their relevance in modern hand reading has hugely diminished. However, it's important to understand their significance, as they have an influence on any marking or line that appears on them. For example, if the head line plunges deep into the Lunar mount, this means that a person mentally takes on the lunar traits of moodiness, a strong imagination, a love of mystery and a sense of their inner depths. Alternatively, if the fate line terminates on the Saturn mount, this means that a person's lifepath will be governed by the Saturnian attitudes of commitment, loyalty and sense of duty.

Learning the meanings of the various mounts will enable you to interpret the lines and other markings more accurately. Generally, the palm mounts need to have a line or marking on them to be of any consequence, otherwise you can ignore them. However, there are exceptions. If either the Venus, Lunar or Outer Mars mounts are exaggerated in size, they affect the consciousness of a person whether there are markings on them or not.

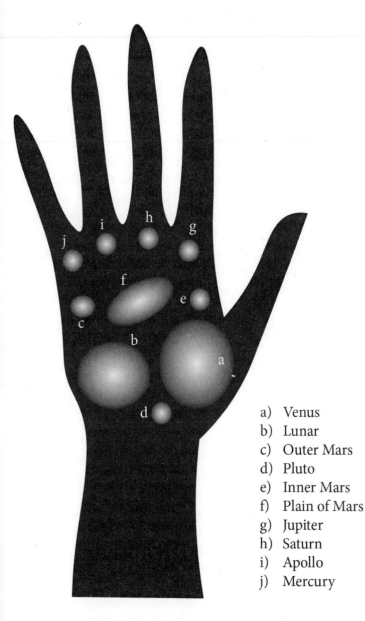

a) Venus
b) Lunar
c) Outer Mars
d) Pluto
e) Inner Mars
f) Plain of Mars
g) Jupiter
h) Saturn
i) Apollo
j) Mercury

VENUS MOUNT

This large, fleshy mount protects the major veins and nerves that connect the hand to the rest of the body. Its size and firmness are general indicators of lust for life, capacity for human warmth and physical resources. When this mount is large and well padded, it's likely that the person has a great capacity to enjoy themselves and will be vigorous, warm, generous, physical and energetic. Often an enlarged Venus mount indicates the need to really embrace life in a full and lusty manner. When it is soft, flat or spongy, there may be a certain lassitude present – the person can lack energy and vitality. This mount will develop as the subject develops muscularity – for example, by going to the gym regularly.

LUNAR MOUNT

Sometimes this area rises into a full, rounded swelling (although it's never as well developed as the Venus mount), or else it bulges outward at the ulnar side of the palm. The Lunar mount deals with our collective subconscious, our moods, our deepest inner yearnings, dreams and imagination. This area is about non-rational, intuitive promptings and our most profound sensibilities. If it's enlarged, there's a love of nature, the past, the sea and anything that inspires the inner world, be it antiques, meditation, music, mystery or any of the arts. If there are signs of sensitivity on the palm (for example, silky skin texture or a water-shaped hand) then there is the strong likelihood that the person has intuitive qualities.

OUTER MARS MOUNT

The Outer Mars mount sometimes bulges outward, giving a curved shape to the ulnar side of the palm. This swelling indicates a pushy, martial, enthusiastic character who has a zeal for advancing their own projects and ideas. Such people are unstoppable if you try to stand against them. It's very common on competitive sportspeople.

PLUTO MOUNT

The Pluto mount (also known as the Neptune mount) is primarily concerned with change and transformation. It is only important when a line moves over it — and in such a case it is almost always the beginning of the fate line or a travel line, both of which indicate change and the impetus to transform one's fortunes (see pages 70 and 83). Travel lines always cross the Pluto mount and give the inclination to branch out and to explore. If the fate line starts on this mount, it means there's a push to find your purpose in life at an early stage.

INNER MARS MOUNT

When a line begins here (usually the head line, but sometimes the life line), it shows physical or mental toughness and the desire to take on any challenge, battle or argument. There is normally a fascination with fitness and sport. Often a line on the Inner Mars mount displays a sense of being threatened and a likelihood of overreacting to any perceived criticism or attack.

PLAIN OF MARS

The plain of Mars, which is never raised and is therefore not considered a mount, is simply an area where there is a sense of realizing projects and advancing oneself. When this plain is crossed by a strong, clear head line, it's a sign of an assertive individual who is astute and successful in their dealings with the world.

JUPITER MOUNT

If there is a line within the Jupiter mount, the person may be battling with issues of ambition, personal power, control, authority and ideals.

SATURN MOUNT

A line in the Saturn mount indicates issues with values, restrictions, rules, contracts, career and the serious life commitments we decide to make, such as marriage and raising a family.

APOLLO MOUNT

Apollo is the Roman god relating to the arts and represents the drive to show off or to seek an audience. Taking after its namesake, lines in the Apollo mount are connected with cultural interests, self-aggrandizement and self-expression.

MERCURY MOUNT

A line in the Mercury mount relates to commerce, communication, eloquence, deception, sexual sophistication and wit.

LEARNING POINTS

When taking a first impression of a person's hands, consider their size, span, colour and texture

The active hand reveals the outer, mature personality, and the passive hand presents the deep, hidden personality

The older a person is, the more their active hand represents their character

Skin texture on the inside of the palm is an important measure of someone's sensitivity and awareness — and there are four types: silk, paper, grainy and coarse

Making hand prints can be a great skill to learn as they show more details about a person's hands

The palm is split down the middle into the radial and ulnar sides

Hands can also be categorized into elemental shapes, but this only works in 70 per cent of people

The mounts are not important unless there is a line or a marking on them. The exception is the size of the Venus, Lunar or Outer Mars areas

The mounts are named after the planets and the moon: Venus, Lunar, Outer Mars, Pluto, Inner Mars, plain of Mars, Jupiter, Saturn, Apollo and Mercury

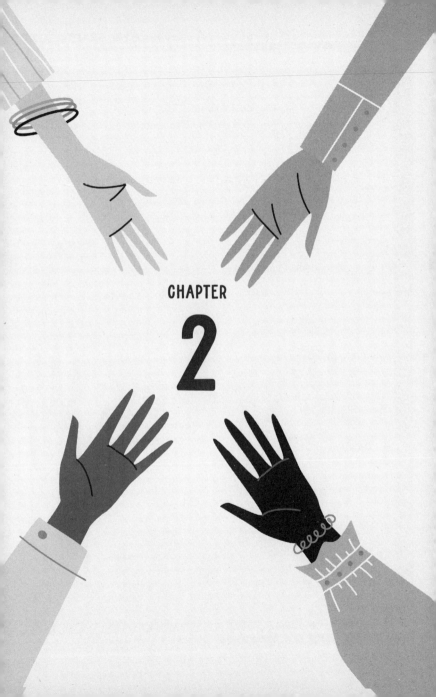

CHAPTER

2

GETTING TO KNOW
THE FINGERS

Once you've explored the hand, it's now time to think about the fingers in more detail. There has been an enormous amount of scientific research in recent years on the implications of the length and balance of the fingers. Anthropologists, psychologists and researchers have proven conclusively that relative finger development reflects health, psychology and behaviour (see Further Reading at the back of the book).

The fingers' relative lengths are shaped by environmental factors, hormonal exposure in the womb and nurturing experiences, so they are powerful indicators of our personality and upbringing.

The fingers are allocated the same planet-inspired names as the mounts below them:

★ **The index finger** is controlled by Jupiter, which in turn rules the ego, sense of control, ambition, personal values and authority.

★ **The middle finger** is named after Saturn, which is about conformity, normality, acceptance of norms, work, religion and attitude to society.

★ **The ring finger** is named the Apollo finger, which indicates our need to be on stage in life, the capacity to take risks, sense of fun, art and culture.

★ **The little finger** is controlled by Mercury, which rules communication, articulacy, ability with language, wit, commerce and sex.

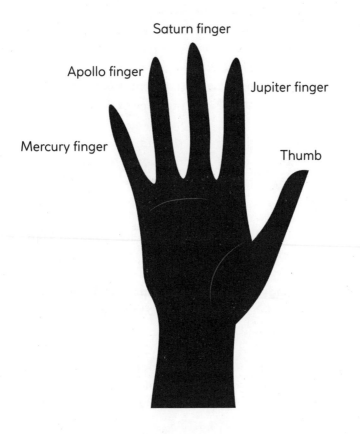

Saturn finger

Apollo finger

Jupiter finger

Mercury finger

Thumb

FIRST IMPRESSIONS

Fingers may differ enormously in their relative or overall length, the space between them and their flexibility. Here are six things I want you to focus on when trying to get a first impression of your hands, and those of your friends and family.

LENGTH

First, how long are the person's fingers? To establish finger length, look at the back of the hand with all the fingers bent forward at a 90-degree angle. Measure the distance from the highest point of the knuckle of the middle finger to the tip of that digit. Then look at the inside palm and measure the distance between the base of the middle finger and the bottom

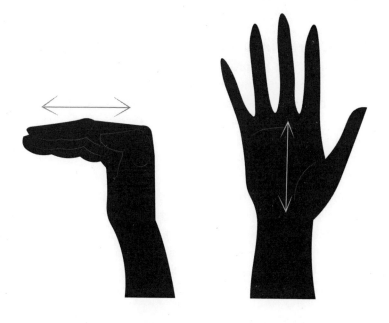

of the palm. Compare these two lengths. If the middle finger is as long as (or longer than) the palm length, the fingers are long. If the middle finger is shorter than the palm length, the fingers are short.

Short fingers are a sign that the person's thought processes are fast and holistic and that they make intuitive guesses and quick judgements. Short-fingered people are uninterested in analysis, pedantic detail or knowledge for its own sake. Instead, they want to hone in on the key facts.

Long fingers indicate the person has thorough, analytical thought processes and takes much longer to act than those with short fingers. They are likely to be specialists in a particular subject, such as consultants, advisors, academics or writers.

SPACE BETWEEN THE DIGITS
If the fingers are naturally held wide apart so there's a 2cm (1in) gap between them and the thumb is held at an angle of 90 degrees, this signifies an open, extrovert personality, but if the fingers and thumb are held close together, a closed, introverted nature is indicated.

FLEXIBILITY
If someone has digits that won't bend back at all when you pull on them, they have stiff fingers, which indicates they have a lot of repressed fear or anger and a rigid approach to life. People with stiff fingers are very strong-minded and psychologically inflexible. On the other hand, if their digits bend back when you pull on them, they have flexible fingers. The further they

bend back, and thus the more flexible they are, the more they indicate spontaneous, fluid and erratic thought processes. Often the other joints of the body are also highly flexible. This is the sign of an inspired, open mind, but one that may lack application and focus.

THE PHALANGES

Each finger is separated into three sections, known as phalanges. Sometimes the higher, middle or lower phalanges stand out by being unusually fleshy and well developed, or they might be thin and wasted. The size of each phalange can indicate important aspects of a person's values.

The lower sections on each finger are the sensual phalanges. When these are especially large and full, the taste, touch and pleasure senses are heightened. This characteristic is found among chocoholics, wine tasters, gastronomes, masseurs and anyone who loves the pleasures of the flesh. If the lower phalanges are narrow and underdeveloped, it indicates an ascetic personality.

higher

middle

lower

The middle sections on each finger are the executive phalanges. Sometimes these are longer and plumper than the others. This is associated with organization, planning, being active and directing mental energy. Large middle phalanges are found in effective, hard-working, skilful people who are great managers and strategists. On the other hand, if the middle phalanges are short and thin, this can be a sign of weak executive ability, poor application and an inability to complete projects.

The higher phalanges represent the abstract realm. If these are particularly large, it reveals a fascination with philosophy, ideals, concepts and spiritual notions. However, if the higher phalanges are small, it shows a lack of interest in these higher concepts.

KNOTTY FINGERS

Sometimes the fingers have little bulges around the joints. These are easy to see as knotty fingers tend to make the phalanges look waisted in at the centre as the knots bulge out. Knobbly fingers with pronounced knots at the joints (that are not a result of arthritis) reflect a pedantic, critical, thorough and exacting way of thinking. Knots show rational, studious qualities in the personality, and a lack of spontaneity.

THE FINGERS' INCLINATIONS

Fingers often bend or lean toward another finger – this is called their inclination, and it betrays a bend or leaning in an individual's psychology. Obviously, a bend in a digit shows a deeper, more fixed attitude than when a finger merely leans in one direction or another. Look at how the fingers on your hands, or your friend's hands, are inclined and see what this means.

The most common inclination of a digit is when the index finger bends or leans toward the middle finger. This indicates a need for support and is often a sign of materialism. The person lacks independence and depends too heavily on work, society and convention to give them a sense of who they are. If the index finger leans or bends *away* from the middle finger, this shows independence – personal freedom is more important to them than duty and responsibility.

The middle finger sometimes leans or bends toward the ring finger. This indicates a sort of "wrong-headedness", an attitude that's unconventional. Often the person's timing in major life decisions (for example, changing jobs or having children) is unusual and they are out of step with society. They tend to lean toward alternative ways of living, and they often want to escape the world of work and duty.

Sometimes a finger has a pronounced bend toward another. It might be the ring finger that is leaning or bending toward the middle finger. This shows that the person is too self-sacrificing and that their pleasures and free time are given over to the demands of work, duty or family.

If the middle and ring digits are bent toward one another, the person may have a martyr complex – the individual may feel that they are carrying the weight of the world on their shoulders and there's never enough time to explore their own inclinations. It's also a sign of stifled creativity.

The little finger often bends toward the ring digit. This reveals a predisposition to bend the truth and a great capacity for flattery, diplomacy and manipulation of words. In some professions (such as sales and law), this can be a huge advantage. If the little finger bends or leans *away* from the ring digit, this indicates a need to explore unusual ideas and a desire to hide one's private life.

RELATIVE FINGER POSITIONS

As far as finger setting is concerned, it is common for the Mercury (little) finger to be set lower in the hand. This makes the Mercury finger appear short, when in fact it's of normal length but sunk deeper into the body of the palm. Look at the image opposite and compare the low-set Mercury finger with the normal finger position. When the lower phalange crease is in line with the base of the ring digit (as shown in the hand on the right), it can be a sign of sexual immaturity and shows that the person's father figure might have been physically or emotionally absent, or that this relationship was far too dependent and close. Since it can take this person years to fully understand their own emotional motivations, they should avoid marrying or having children too early.

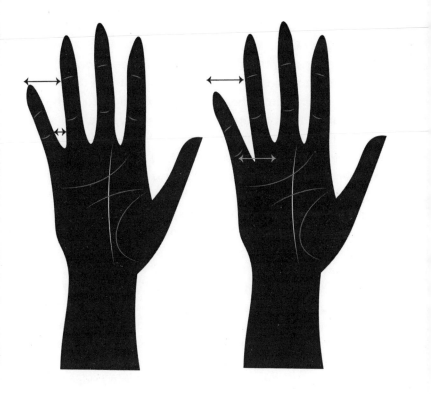

LENGTH AND ATTRIBUTES OF THE INDIVIDUAL FINGERS

After you have finished taking first impressions of the fingers, it's vital to focus on any digits that you have identified as longer or shorter than average. This reveals powerful motivations within the psyche, which affect the individual's behaviour very strongly and are a key clue to the kind of upbringing they've had.

JUPITER FINGER

The most important digit is the index finger, known as the Jupiter digit. It's measured by comparing it with the ring finger. If you lay a ruler across the tips of these two digits (pushing the middle finger back to keep it out of the way) you can easily see which is longer. If the index finger is the same length or a fraction — no more than 3mm (⅒in) — shorter, it can be considered average. If the index finger is smaller by more than 3mm (⅒in), it's short. If the Jupiter finger is longer than the ring finger by even the tiniest margin, it's considered long. A long or short Jupiter finger is highly significant.

Imagine this finger as a mirror, reflecting the individual's sense of power, authority and importance. If it's long, this shows a heightened sense of responsibility, authority and need for control, and a bossy, idealistic attitude to life. People with this characteristic are perfectionists. They have high personal values and a constantly nagging conscience. They are extremely proud and take themselves seriously. A long Jupiter finger shows that the childhood of the individual was marked by an overriding sense of duty because the mother figure was either absent or overpowering.

When the Jupiter digit is short, the person has a diminished sense of self-importance and deep feelings of inadequacy. It can be an indicator that their childhood rarely reinforced their sense of personal accountability and power. Due to this, there is a danger that the person will lack the sense of responsibility required to achieve their goals. Those with short Jupiter fingers often overcompensate and appear self-aggrandizing, but this is just an act. People with this characteristic never take themselves too seriously. Self-neglect (for example, poor diet or alcoholism) has been linked to this digit being extremely short, so it may be appropriate to gently raise this and encourage the person to address any such issues.

SATURN FINGER

The Saturn (middle) finger's length is measured by drawing a line across the tips of the neighbouring index and ring digits, and observing how much the middle finger projects above this line. It is normal for the line to cross just over halfway up the higher phalange of the Saturn finger. You can check by looking at the back of the palm. Three-quarters of the nail on the middle finger should stand above the tips of the neighbouring digits.

A long Saturn digit shows that the person is hard-working and a pillar of society, usually inclined toward structured, traditional professions, such as medicine, law, local government, the armed forces, administration or management.

A short Saturn finger often indicates a person that rebels and leads an alternative lifestyle. This is a sign of someone who distrusts authority, and it is common among artists, anarchists, travellers and unconventional, alternative types.

APOLLO FINGER

The Apollo (ring) finger indicates the development of the persona, the public face. It's linked to the peacock-like drive to draw attention to oneself, a remnant of the competitive instinct to attract a mate. Looking at this finger will indicate their need for adulation, engagement in the arts and every form of creative expression. This digit is measured by comparing it to the Jupiter (index) finger.

People with a long Apollo digit may take risks and worry too much about their looks and popularity. Show business and the stage are dominated by people with long ring fingers. While there's a strong need for self-expression, it's not always under a spotlight. If the palm is also a water type, or the skin is silky, self-expression may take a gentle, collective form such as being a member of a choir.

If the Apollo finger is short, creativity and popularity are less important than integrity and self-respect. For people with short Apollo fingers, control is paramount to performance and the person's art is usually centred on their own experience.

MERCURY FINGER
The Mercury (little) finger represents all aspects of communication, including body language, nuance, wit, verbal dexterity and innuendo. It also governs money and sexual intimacy. The average length is for the tip to come up to the highest crease line on the neighbouring (Apollo) finger. If the Mercury finger comes above this crease line, it is considered longer than average, and likewise anything shorter is considered shorter than average.

If their Mercury digit is longer than this crease line, the person has fluency and a love of language, the capacity to articulate deeper feelings, and financial acumen. People who work in education, sales, finance and comedy tend to have a long Mercury finger.

When the Mercury finger is short, the person will have a child-like nature. People who have lots of children or who work with children often have this feature. Those with short Mercury fingers sometimes find it difficult to express their deeper needs and feelings and may have a love of sentimental music and TV shows. Often they are uncertain with their finances.

THUMB

The thumb, while not technically a finger, is still important in palmistry as it indicates will power, self-control and personal drive. The thumb is like a rudder — its length and flexibility can be used as a gauge for the person's capacity to steer toward their goals and attainments. The longer and stiffer the thumb, the more strength a person has to master personal circumstances. For this reason, the thumb is always long and stiff in athletes and self-made business people.

The length of the thumb is measured by laying it against the neighbouring Jupiter (index) digit. The tip should reach anywhere between one third to halfway up the first phalange of this digit. A thumb that reaches higher than this point indicates high motivation, self-discipline and a dominant personality. A thumb that reaches lower than this point shows limited will and drive. It's best for those with this feature to find a partner with a stronger thumb to motivate and push them to achieve.

Thumb stiffness is checked by bending the thumb back toward the wrist. Usually there are a few centimetres of flexibility, but sometimes the thumb will bend almost to the wrist. When it won't bend back at all, it's a stiff thumb. Bendy-thumbed types hate applying themselves to tough, disciplined regimes, and tend to be artists, actors and musicians. Such people are friendly, open and change plans on impulse. Stiff-thumbed people, however, apply themselves rigorously to a task. They are found in any situation where a strong work ethic is required.

FOCUS ON THE FINGERTIPS

Now that you know the attributes of each finger, it's time to zoom in on the fingertips.

FINGERTIP SHAPES

Generally, the fingertips are rounded — this is normal and average. However, sometimes the fingertips are square, pointed or spatulate (wedge shaped); each of these shapes indicate a certain mode of self-expression. If most of the fingertips are square, this demonstrates a practical, ordered, nit-picking attitude. Everything is put in its proper place. People with pointed tips are impractical, dreamy and spiritually

square   spatulate   rounded   pointed

or philosophically inclined. Spatulate tips, where the finger widens at the end, are found on people who are passionate, energetic, impatient and intense.

FINGERNAILS

Modern palmistry no longer regards fingernail shape as indicative of personality. However, nails are still a useful indicator of general health. Healthy nails are light pink with a gentle lustre. Red nails indicate high blood pressure or other circulatory problems. Blue nails show a likely cardiovascular disorder. Yellow nails mark possible liver problems and pale nails can be a sign of anaemia. If someone has white specks on their nails, they may be suffering with high levels of stress or mineral deficiency. Fine, longitudinal ridges are associated with overactive adrenals, rheumatic illness or thyroid imbalance. Horizontal ridges occur if accident or illness temporarily halts growth. Bulbous nails indicate respiratory problems and brittle nails reveal vitamin and mineral deficiency.

FINGERPRINTS

Fingerprints are an exciting aspect of modern hand reading. Until 50 years ago, hand readers had no inkling that fingerprints were of any importance. However, scientific research has made startling connections between print patterns and specific mindsets and thought processes. The patterns on our fingertips show the patterns of our mental reasoning and add enormously to the array of tools we have as palmists. Palmists identify different personality traits from reading the whole palm but the fingerprints can often reveal our most unconscious thinking patterns.

There can be no more personal and unique symbol of you than your fingerprints. The police use fingerprinting to try to identity the perpetrators of crime; the Chinese authorities were using hand prints in crime scene investigations as early as the Qin Dynasty (221–206 BC). A common misconception is that identical twins have the same fingerprints, but in fact fingerprints are formed before birth and minute environmental differences, such as the position of each fetus in the womb, affect the patterns that are formed. Fingerprints can often be one of the only differences between two identical twins. The fact that fingerprints are unique to each individual means that, even today, in many parts of the world a thumbprint is used instead of a signature for those who are illiterate.

Fingerprints never change their pattern although they may fade a little as the skin thins with age. While lines may show how family, upbringing, environment and other factors affect your personality, they will change over time as your life and behaviour, beliefs and attitudes changes. Your fingerprints are unchanging and show the inherent characteristic traits you have and the parameters within which your psyche operates. However, this information – as with all elements of palm reading – must be taken in the context of the whole reading and not as a stand-alone feature.

They are unique to each person but fall into six basic types, albeit with minor variations. These six print patterns are:

★ Ulnar loop

★ Radial loop

★ Composite loop

★ Whorl

★ Simple arch

★ Tented arch

Ulnar loop

Radial loop

Composite loop

Whorl

Simple arch

Tented arch

Most (around $2/3$) of the patterns you see on the fingers will be ulnar loops. When you see ulnar loops (either with the naked eye or under a magnifying glass), don't bother analyzing them, since this pattern is so common it is rather meaningless. Any prints *other* than ulnar loops, though, are powerful psychological indicators. Always discuss with the person you're reading the issues raised when you see a non-ulnar-loop print anywhere on their hand.

Over the next few pages we'll be looking at how to identify all six patterns, what each one indicates and how their location can impact this meaning.

THE SIX PRINT PATTERNS

Now let's work our way through the prints on the digits and on the thumb, examining the traits shown by the most common print variances.

ULNAR LOOP
This is the most common pattern, and thus is ignored in a reading. The ulnar loop forms a wave shape, flowing toward the thumb, and indicates a "go with the flow" mentality. It makes for one who is empathic, gregarious, adaptable, receptive and impressionable, with a need to belong.

RADIAL LOOP
This is the same pattern as the ulnar loop but facing the opposite direction, flowing away from the thumb rather than toward it. Radial loops are much rarer than ulnar loops and

are usually found on the Jupiter (index) finger. This pattern can be found on people that are hyper-receptive to others and unduly sensitive to criticism. It can make for a highly defensive personality, one with a lot of insecurities and a strong need for positive responses from others. Radial loops are sometimes called "carers' loops" as they are so often found on professional carers.

COMPOSITE LOOP
The composite print is formed by two loops facing in opposite directions. This reveals cycles of enthusiasm, disappointment and moodiness. The person is mentally never certain of anything and there is a constant duality in the mind from this sign of two prints in one. In Eastern societies the composite is seen as a spiritual indication. There is always difficulty in making life decisions. Composite loops reflect a wise, anti-fanatic, universal viewpoint.

WHORL
The whorl is formed of a series of ever-decreasing circles or a spiral formation. One variation on the whorl is called a peacock's eye, where its circles are trapped within a loop. A whorl can be found on someone original, secretive and studious, with no group mentality. The whorl print reflects a need for space and freedom; it is a sign of someone individual, talented, secretive, self-motivated and self-centred.

SIMPLE ARCH
This is formed from an almost flat chevron formation of lines piled on top of one another. A simple arch reflects a deep,

fixed, materialistic, stubborn attitude to life. People with one or more simple arches are very loyal, emotionally repressed, faithful, persistent, practical and unassuming.

TENTED ARCHES

These form a sharp spike pointing skyward. This pattern reflects the impulse to shock, surprise and impress. It drives the need to break out of boundaries, to be prominent, to be noticed. The tented arch presents a character that is enthusiastic, fanatical, excitable, intense, restless and, in some ways, extreme.

THE EFFECT OF EACH PRINT ON THE INDIVIDUAL FINGERS

The composite loop, radial loop, whorl and simple and tented arches vary their meaning according to which finger they're on. The most common variances are listed here. Some are not mentioned as they are incredibly rare; for example, a tented arch is found on only one in 2,600 Mercury fingers.

JUPITER FINGERPRINTS

Radial loop: This shows that the person is insecure, desperate to please, a carer and a people person. They are prickly about criticism, great flatterers, highly sociable and find it hard to say no.

Composite loop: This is a sign of perennial doubt about ideals, identity and goals. The person is philosophical, impartial, always able to see others' viewpoints and a good judge or counsellor.

Whorl: This indicates difficulty in feeling part of a group. The person likes to operate and work alone, is secretive, original and eccentric, and needs space and freedom.

Simple arch: The person is pragmatic, family orientated and obstinate, dislikes pretension, and is predictable, fond of routine, fiercely loyal, materialistic and repressed.

Tented arch: This denotes an excitable, enthusiastic, dramatic, idealistic, creative and restless nature. Those with a tented arch need drama in their lives.

SATURN FINGERPRINTS

Radial loop: This person is insecure about the right lifestyle and career to follow. They are extremely open to different cultures and ways of living, and adapt easily to new experiences. The person may have a tendency to overconform or be highly rebellious.

Composite loop: This person is always uncertain about being in the right career and often changes their spiritual and philosophical views. They are open to other cultures and beliefs.

Whorl: The person may be fascinated by non-conformist beliefs, lifestyles and people, and could often decide to go against the rules. They are obsessed with freedom, both personal and societal, and hate any and all repressive regimes.

Simple arch: This shows someone who opts for a secure, well-paid career. They have a strong sense of fairness and justice and are fascinated by the past, the natural and the traditional.

APOLLO FINGERPRINTS

Whorl: This denotes a gift for design, colour and style. The person may be original in their choice of clothes and in the arts. The whorl also shows good spatial skills and a talent for ball games.

Simple arch: The person is inclined toward physical activities and sports, and loves crafts or any aesthetic that could be termed primitive, naturalistic or historical.

MERCURY FINGERPRINTS

Whorl: This denotes a secretive and studious person with obscure interests and specialist knowledge in an unusual field. They are likely to marry someone who is very different from themselves in terms of age, culture or background.

Simple arch: This often indicates the person is involved in teaching or helping infants or adults in basic learning skills. The roots and nature of communication are important to them. They are markedly reluctant to discuss their intimate life.

THUMB PRINTS

Composite loop: The person may struggle to make personal commitments due to their stop–go attitude. The person is easily persuaded or dissuaded and can see two sides to every decision. There is always duality in life decisions.

Whorl: This shows a self-starter — someone who operates alone, loves new concepts and innovations, is original in their approach and has their own way of doing things.

Simple arch: The person is pragmatic, systematic, stubborn, thorough and practical. This feature is often a sign of manual skill and of scepticism about lofty ideals.

LEARNING POINTS

When taking a first impression of a person's fingers, consider their length, the space between digits, flexibility, phalanges, inclinations and finger positions

Each finger is separated into three phalanges — the sensual, the executive and the abstract realm

The direction a finger leans or bends displays deep psychological learnings

The little finger is sometimes set low, showing a slow awakening of a sense of maturity in relationships

The Jupiter finger is the most important, as it's a reflection of the ego, the sense of authority and personal power

The Saturn finger should project above the other fingers by almost half the higher phalange

The thumbs are about self-control and will power

The fingerprints are powerful pointers to character and are a relatively new aspect of modern hand reading

On average, fingertips are rounded, but they can also be square, pointed or spatulate

Ideally, the fingernails are light pink in colour with visible moons and no ridges, white specks, or brittleness

There are six patterns of note in fingerprints: ulnar loop, radial loop, composite loop, whorl, simple arch and tented arch

It is important to consider on which finger each pattern appears, as this alters the meaning

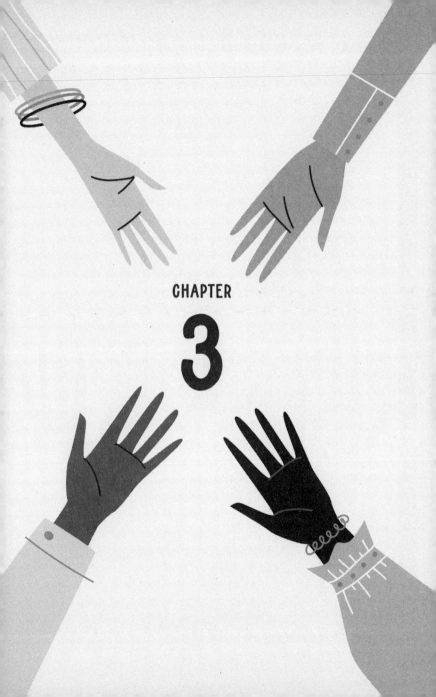

CHAPTER

3

THE MAJOR LINES

There are four major lines on the palm: the life line, heart line, head line and fate line. These are almost always present in some form on everyone's hand. This chapter will also show you the Simian line, which is the merging of the head and heart lines.

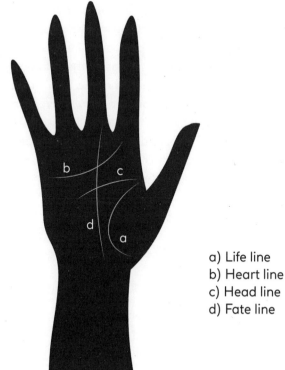

a) Life line
b) Heart line
c) Head line
d) Fate line

The major lines illustrate the person's physical, emotional, intellectual and directional drives. Each line is like a major highway of energy. A line that's long, clear and deep indicates strong, vigorous energy. A line that's weak, broken or short shows that a person is functioning poorly in that area. The major lines will change slowly over time. It is normal to have at least one major line that is of less than optimum quality.

You should always read the lines in the context of the palm they are marked on. This is very important. If the fate line (which represents one's goals, dedication and direction in life) is completely missing on an earth palm with coarse skin, the nature of the earth person is to plod on in life in a traditional manual role, following in the footsteps of the parents, so this may not be a problem. However, if the fate line is missing on an air palm with paper skin, the person will overthink their options, continually dither in life direction, try 38 different vocations, spend an awful lot of time in the wrong type of work and become very frustrated. This is why it's vital to always consider the broader issues in the palm when judging the lines.

A hand covered with lots of scratchy lines is an indication of a stressed, nervous disposition. A hand with only the four major lines on it shows someone who is calm, focused and uncomplicated.

LIFE LINE

The life line begins above the thumb and runs downward, forming a semicircle around the Venus mount, ending at the palm base. This line represents physicality, vigour, energy, stamina, sense of security and stability. It also represents homeostasis (the regulation of bodily processes), and the amount of regenerative energy available.

A complete, deeply etched line reveals high stamina, vitality and energy, and shows that a person has their feet firmly on the ground. A strong line means that the main structures of life are sound.

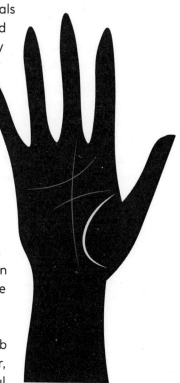

A short, weak, faint line on the active hand indicates a perennial sense of insecurity, an unstable lifestyle, a fearful attitude, poor energy or a sense of feeling unsupported. Stress levels are likely to be high. If the life line is weak and broken on the passive hand, this is a sign of an insecure background, where stable family structures were not reinforced.

If the life line hugs the ball of the thumb tightly, staying under the Jupiter finger, this is a sign of a restricted, fearful personality. However, if the line swings out toward the centre of the palm, it's a sign of boldness — this person jumps in with both feet, always seeking new experiences.

If the life line is broken at any point, this signals that the stability of a person's life will be, or has been, interrupted. This may take the form of a divorce, emigration, illness or some such disruptive event. Check the quality of the line after the break — if it's stronger, life is getting better; if the line is weaker, the person will take a longer time to recover. It's a myth that a short life line indicates a short life. In fact, people with short life lines often embark on fanatic health regimes because of their innate insecurity and end up living longer than most!

You can time a marking on the life line by assuming the full length to the base of the palm is 90 years, halfway down is 45 years and so on. When you see a break or weakness on the life line, always advise the person to establish regular, healthy diet, sleep and exercise routines and a stable home life. Over time this will repair any weak or broken line.

Chained lines are like a series of bubbles forming a rough line. Islands (chain links) on the line indicate periods of lowered energy and uncertainty — they often appear in the run-up to divorce, bankruptcy or family crisis. Again, good health routines will help.

Lines originating from within the Venus mount that cross the life line indicate stress from family and the home. Small lines reaching up toward the Jupiter digit on the upper part of the life line are effort lines. The longer and stronger the effort lines, the more a person feels motivated to achieve — a sign of a successful, ambitious temperament.

Occasionally the life line is doubled, with the two lines running parallel to each other. This shows a dynamic, travel-orientated personality — someone who belongs to two bases, countries or cultures.

HEART LINE

The heart line is an indicator not only of the capacity to love, connect and form relationships, but also of our ability to emote. If this line is of poor quality, it will impact the subject's ability to experience joy, or to be transported by nature, beauty, art or spirituality. If this line is missing completely (an extremely rare occurrence), the person will have problems with expressing emotion and relating to others.

The heart line begins under the Mercury digit, running below the fingers and ending anywhere beneath the Jupiter or Saturn fingers. The line can be straight, or it can curve up or, occasionally, down.

The quality of the line corresponds to the emotional state of the individual. Weak, broken lines with small islands show that the person can't put their whole heart into relationships and that their emotions are complex and muddled. People with a poor-quality heart line feel disconnected and are easily hurt. Engaging with performance arts such as dance and music will improve a weak line quite quickly.

People with straight heart lines are emotionally straightforward. They aren't romantic in a gushing, expressive, idealistic sense but are more practical and considered. If the line is straight and ends below the Saturn digit, the person is emotionally undemonstrative, and when in a relationship will focus chiefly on fidelity, finance and other practical matters. A person with a straight heart line ending beneath the Jupiter digit demonstrates love by means of gifts and actions. There's a marked reluctance to indulge in emotional "scenes" with outpourings of tears and rage. If a straight heart line crosses the palm from under the Mercury finger all the way to under the Jupiter finger, it's a sign that the person sacrifices one-to-one relationships in favour of the needs of others. This is common in carers, healers, doctors and therapists; such people often take on damaged or needy partners.

People with heart lines that curve upward are expressive, effusive and demonstrative. If the line curves up to the Saturn digit, the person is expressive, but somewhat unadventurous romantically. If the line curves up to the Jupiter digit, an idealistic, over-romantic nature is revealed, and love is tinted by personal visions and expectations. All too often a partner is placed on an impossibly high pedestal, only to tumble back to earth. A heart line ending between the middle and index digits is perhaps a good balance of expression and idealism.

Heart lines that curve downward show an expectation or actual experience of romantic loss and a reluctance to express themselves in traditional gender roles, both in appearance and manner. Downward branching forks that taper off the end of the heart line show disappointment and loss, and jealousy is often an issue if the branch continues downward near or onto the life line.

Broken-off sections of the heart line, which float above the end of the line, show an ability to express an upbeat, passionate nature, but only when in public. It's quite common to see multiple endings to the heart line. For example, there might be a broken-off section floating above the end of the line, with a dropping section reaching toward the life line and a branch moving toward the Jupiter finger. This shows the confusion and complexity of modern emotional lives, with repressed insecurity, fake effusiveness and romanticism all muddled together.

Ironically, a clear, long, upward-curved heart line is often found on those that are long-term singletons, while a poor-quality line is seen on those permanently in some form of attachment. The reason for this is that those with strong lines are deeply emotive and expressive and are willing to wait, possibly for years, for the partner who resonates and reflects their own passions. Those with poor, broken, islanded and otherwise weaker heart lines crave emotional connection and find it difficult to be alone; they compensate for this by staying in (sometimes unsatisfying) relationships.

HEAD LINE

The head line is a hugely significant indicator of the way we think and how we process information. The quality of the line illustrates mental focus. If the line is fuzzy, broken and weak, the mind functions in an unclear, distracted manner. If the line is clear and sharp, it indicates highly focused mental processes.

The head line begins near the top of the life line and runs across the middle of the palm. Sometimes, it even begins joined to the life line. If the head line is bonded to the life line for more than 2cm (¾in), this shows low confidence, caution and an unwillingness to step outside the familiar. The person may allow others to decide things for them. On the passive hand, this is a sign of domineering parents. Alternatively, if there's a gap of more than 1cm (½in) between the top of the life line and the start of the head line, this indicates independence and confidence in one's opinions, high aspirations and high-mindedness. Often a large gap shows someone that's elevated themselves to great heights in life.

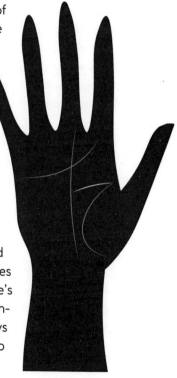

The longer the head line, the more time a person spends speculating before making a decision. If the head line runs straight and level across the palm all the way to the other side, this indicates an unsentimental, analytical nature, high intelligence and nervous tension. People with long, straight lines (ending under the Mercury finger) are philosophical, objective, rational and far-seeing, speculating endlessly over possibilities. Consultants almost always have long head lines. Individuals who have short, straight head lines that do not go beyond the Saturn finger are decisive, pragmatic and action-orientated – they are excellent at putting all their energies into their career and goals. With limited interest in the intellect but enormous commitment to applying ideas and getting things done, they are doers first and thinkers later.

People with bent head lines are more flexible, imaginative and irrational than those with straight ones. Their minds are more fluid, and they see various ways of approaching a problem. They understand that the truth is often a matter of perspective. A head line that bends into the top of the Lunar mount is a sign of a creative, flexible approach. This shows an individual who will put a lot of personal vision into projects and goals, and their actions and surroundings reflect a sense of flair. Their mental outlook is sentimental, shaped by emotions and drawing on dreams and memories. When the head line is *very* bent, curving sharply downward to the base of the Lunar mount, this signals a strongly subjective view of other people and the world in general. This person is great at responding to the emotional content of poetry or delving into the deeper realms of the soul, but can be deeply moody and introverted.

They can harbour past grievances and also lack objectivity and level-headedness.

Forks at the end of the head line show creative flair and inspiration in ideas. They reveal a broader aspect to the personality.

If the head lines on the active and passive hands are remarkably different, there may be a surprising disparity between the inner and outer personalities. Always look at the head line in conjunction with the skin texture, palm shape and finger length. If you're studying an earth hand with coarse skin and short fingers, then it doesn't matter whether the head line is long and clear: you have a hardy, practical, outdoors person, uninterested in the nuances of academia.

After you have looked at the head line, I would always recommend taking some time to compare the head line with the heart line. If the heart line is stronger, deeper and more marked in the palm than the head line, the emotions dominate the personality. No matter how fine and clear the head line, there will be times when the person is highly irrational. A dominant heart line indicates that thought processes will be strongly affected by passions and feelings. On the other hand, if the head line is stronger then the person is ruled by their head instead of their heart.

Islands are not often seen on the head line, but when present they indicate that a person is stressed, psychologically fragile and easily overloaded. It is often the sign of someone with high mental function who's a specialist in a particular area, but who can become slightly obsessive and take things out of proportion.

The head line is one of the fastest to change in the palm, whereas the life line is usually the slowest. It's fascinating to watch an island on the head line slowly fade and shrink when the subject goes on a meditation course, or takes a few months off work to combat stress. Similarly, when someone embarks on a course of extensive study, like a university degree, the head line gets noticeably longer.

SIMIAN LINE

Very rarely (on fewer than one per cent of palms) you'll encounter a simian line. This is where the head and heart lines combine to make a single line across the palm. Simian lines are a sign of a single-minded, intense personality with controlled passions — someone who is highly focused. In palmistry it's called the "quietly raging storm". As the head and heart lines are fused, neither the feelings nor the viewpoints can be open and free to express themselves. People with a simian line (known as "simians") put their entire mind and emotions into everything they do and have highly obsessive natures. Usually, simians have phenomenal stamina and an unparalleled drive to achieve things. They can be simultaneously charming and ruthless. Don't be fooled by how they always appear to be very calm and controlled; they always find themselves under great internal pressure.

FATE LINE

The fate line is usually the hardest major line for beginner palmists to spot. It's quite common for this line not to form until a person has matured and is in their twenties. It isn't a problem if this line is missing on a child but it becomes a more serious issue if it's missing on someone in their late twenties or older.

The fate line runs up the centre of the palm toward the base of the Saturn finger. The fate line is often called the "lifepath line", as it's a key indicator as to whether we've found our calling in life. It shows our character, our attitude to work, our personal goals and intentions, and our sense of individuality. If the line's missing, there's little sense of identity or personal goals. There's no commitment and no direction, but rather someone who is motivated by their peers or parents. A faint, weak, fractured line shows that the person hasn't yet found themselves, and they feel unfulfilled. This line develops when a person is separated from formative influences and able to look deep within themselves to discover their passions and intentions.

When the line starts at the base of the palm, it shows that a sense of responsibility began early in life, with an important role outside the home and a strong sense of duty – the classic "old head on young shoulders".

Often the line only starts halfway up the palm, close to the head line. This illustrates a person whose life truly began in their thirties when their work and life directions fell into place. The later the line develops, the longer it took the person to develop a sense of purpose.

If the fate line starts on the Lunar mount, it's a sure sign that the person's work and lifestyle are vastly different from their family's wishes. On the other hand, if the line starts from the life line, it reveals that family will always influence any life decision the individual makes and work will be based on the need for security and stability.

Complete lines that run all the way from the base of the palm to the bottom of the Saturn digit demonstrate an onerous sense of duty. This is the mark of someone who makes life hard for themselves by taking on too much responsibility. It's often found in lawyers, managers, overzealous parents, financial advisors and in the armed and other uniformed services.

Sometimes the fate line is not just a single line but is doubled, with two lines running up the palm side by side. This shows a person who can live out two sides of their personality with two different sets of interests, friends and lifestyles. The further apart the lines, the further apart the two sides of the personality.

LEARNING POINTS

There are four major lines on the palm: life line, heart line, head line and fate line

Strong, deep lines show strong, deep energy whereas weak lines indicate weak energy

The major lines will change over time as we change

Always read the lines in the context of the palm

The life line is about security and stability

The heart line is an indicator of a person's capacity to emote

The head line shows how we mentally process information — if we are level-headed or changeable, intuitive or fact-based

Simian lines are formed when the head and heart lines fuse together in a single line

People with simian lines can be very intense, focused and are often under great pressure

The fate line is the most difficult line to see, and it indicates our values and goals

CHAPTER

4

THE MINOR LINES

The minor lines are much fainter, scratchier and more variable and obscure than the major lines. They indicate specific drives, talents or personality traits that can be especially powerful in a reading. Very few people have all the minor lines in their hands — some people might not even have any. Since they are so individual and show the complexity and uniqueness of human nature, minor lines change very quickly; they can disappear and reappear within a few months.

This chapter will take you through some of the minor lines you might find on a palm during a reading.

APOLLO LINE

The Apollo line is fine and thread-like, running vertically beneath the Apollo finger. This line is almost always visible on the Apollo mount but it's only significant and meaningful in a reading if it extends below the heart line by at least 2.5cm (1in). If it does extend this far, the line can be seen as a gauge of contentment. This is because it only appears when we develop a calm inner life and feel fulfilled with our lot. It's always a positive sign. In fact, the longer the line, the more content the person. Those with a well-developed Apollo line love their own company and often feel connected to a higher realm. It's found on those that become completely absorbed in an activity, usually an art, therapy or wellbeing practice.

INTUITION LINE

The intuition line is very rare. It's a bow-shaped line running up the ulnar side of the palm below the Mercury finger. Signifying intuitive powers, insight and the capacity to see and sense phenomena beyond the strictly rational, it's always present on mediums and psychics.

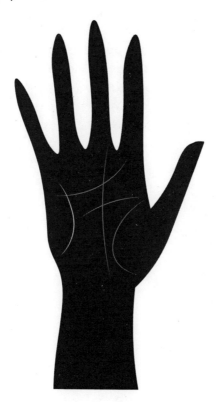

LINE OF MARS

The line of Mars is located within the arc of the life line above the thumb. In nine out of ten cases where the line is present, the line of Mars is weak and short – under 2.5cm (1in) – and this is no cause for concern. However, when the line is long – over 2.5cm (1in) – as well as being red and deep, this shows a competitive, tough streak in an individual's make-up. It gives a muscular, energetic drive, and shows that this person is always up for a challenge. A strong line of Mars is common in sports people, particularly practitioners of martial arts. There's always a sense of wanting to push oneself to the limits when this line is strong. Sometimes there's a fine line connecting the head line and Mars line together; while it's rare, it always indicates an individual who is quick to argue or to take offence.

HEALTH LINE

This is a single line, or series of scratchy lines, running vertically from the base of the palm toward the Mercury mount. It's strongly connected to the activity of the vagus nerve, which regulates digestion and breathing. The health line is almost always poorly formed and deteriorates with age. The deeper and more broken up it is, the more body processes are affected. When (in very rare cases) the line is clear, singular and fine, it's a sign of an inventive, original mind and an excellent mind—body connection. This is common on yoga, tai chi and meditation practitioners, as well as on original thinkers.

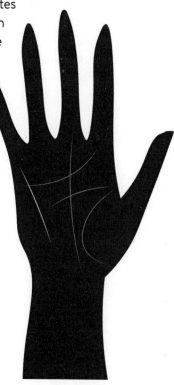

VIA LASCIVIA

This is a curved line that cuts off the base of the Lunar mount. The via lascivia line indicates that a person is drawn to stimulants and to dynamic exercise routines and experiences that give a physical high. It also signals an intense reaction to intoxicants. If you discover this line in a reading, you should advise the person to take an allergy test.

GIRDLE OF VENUS

The girdle of Venus is a horizontal line that floats above the heart line. It's rarely found in complete form and is usually fragmented. It's a sign of a personality that's always in search of higher experiences, whether that is in the form of drink, drugs or parties. On a thick-skinned palm, it may suggest someone who takes part in sensual and sexual experimentation; on a more sensitive, soft-skinned palm, it may indicate someone who loves the arts or who is always trying to attain the heights of perfection. It's always a sign of a love of luxury and the exotic.

Whenever the girdle of Venus appears, it's like a mirage in a person's mind, always drawing them to the magical, the mystical and the exotic. Spiritual seekers and visionaries always have a strong girdle of Venus. The stronger the line, the stronger the need to escape reality, and the harder it is to be confined to the day-to-day world. When the girdle of Venus appears in fragmentary form, it shows a fragmented, nervous disposition, always trying to get high and out of one's mind in some way.

RING OF SOLOMON

The ring of Solomon is a very fine line that encircles the base of the Jupiter digit. This line shows a fascination with psychology and a strong insight into other people's personalities. It is commonly found on the palms of counsellors, psychologists and good listeners.

TRAVEL LINES

Travel lines are branches at the base of the life line, reaching toward the base of the Lunar mount. They commonly appear as multiple lines. Not only do travel lines show an irresistible urge to travel, but they also indicate a need for variety and an unwillingness to be burdened with too many responsibilities that keep one close to home. The more travel lines you see, the more restless the person, although it's rare to see more than three travel lines.

TEACHER'S SQUARE

A teacher's square is not a perfect square, but it's made of four random lines that form a rough square on the Jupiter mount. Such a marking indicates a predisposition to manage people, to inspire and instruct and to get the best from others.

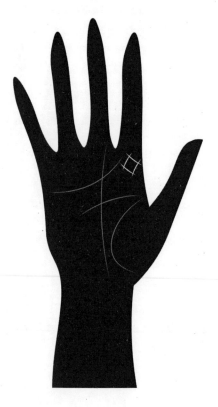

PASSION LINE

The passion line runs up at an angle from the heart line toward the Mercury mount. This line shows a highly visual and imaginative aspect to sexuality. People with this line choose their partners because of their sexual magnetism before anything else. They will always have a colourful sex life – they are more experimental and likely to use, or be fascinated by, erotic imagery or literature. The line doesn't necessarily indicate a high sex drive, but there is always sexual curiosity.

LOOP OF NATURE

The loop of nature is formed when the skin ridges make a loop facing outward on the very edge of the Lunar mount. This indicates a love of the open air and of being close to nature. It has also been linked to the ability to dowse and heal, and a fascination with mystery and things that are hidden.

LOOP OF SENSITIVITY

The loop of sensitivity is found facing inward on the Lunar mount and is quite common. This indicates a heightened awareness — a kind of sixth sense. The person can pick up undercurrents in the atmosphere and is very intuitive in their relationships. This feature is commonly found on the palms of artists, mediums and psychics.

MUSIC LOOP

This uncommon pattern is situated on the base of the Venus mount. It's a squarish loop rising from the base of the Venus mount. The person shows responsiveness to music and rhythm, so musicians and dancers often have this marking.

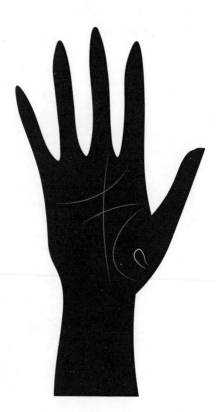

WHORL OF ISOLATION

The whorl of isolation is rare and is situated on the Lunar mount. Bearers of this marking are almost always intensely private and hard to get to know intimately. It can be an indication of eccentricity and the need for space. It's also an artistic sign, as the urge to express one's self creatively often comes from a feeling of being cut off from the world.

MISCELLANEOUS MARKS

You'll often come across random markings such as crosses, stars and other signs that aren't identifiable. Most people have a few of these somewhere on their palm. As a result of the old, superstitious, predictive side of palmistry, random markings often cause great concern and fear. However, their meaning is of minor importance, and they can appear and vanish very quickly. A good example of this are tiny lines on the outer edge of the palm below the Mercury finger. Traditionally, these were signs of how many marriages and children you would have, and many people are still fascinated by them. However, this interpretation, like that of many other marks and patterns, has been proven to be nonsense. It's much more important in a reading to focus on the bigger issues – the hand shape, any fingers that are long or short or any non-ulnar fingerprints.

If you want to examine random markings, you can take a guess at their meaning by their placement. For example, if a marking is on the Jupiter mount, it can only relate to issues of ambition, personal power, authority and ideals. The marking itself gives a hint of its meaning too:

★ **crosses** show two opposing drives or situations and the need to make a decision

★ **dots** show issues caused by inner turmoil

★ **islands** are signs of confusion

Always bear in mind that the hand shape, skin texture, major lines and so on are much more important than these obscure markings, so don't spend too much time on them.

LEARNING POINTS

Minor lines are fainter, scratchier and more variable and obscure than the major lines

Very few people have all the minor lines, and some will have none

The Apollo line is only significant if it runs beneath the heart line for more than 2.5cm (1in)

The intuition line is rare, bow-shaped and reveals intuitive, psychic powers

A strong line of Mars suggests a competitive nature

The health line is often a series of scratchy lines and deteriorates with age, as your health declines

The via lascivia line shows a need for excitement, exercise and an obsession with health

The girdle of Venus is common on artists, fantasists and spiritual seekers as it indicates a need for higher experiences

The ring of Solomon is a sign of a natural counsellor and good listener

Travel lines show a need for travel, change and variety

A teacher's square indicates a natural teacher or manager

The passion line shows a lively sexual imagination and heightened eroticism

The loop of nature is a powerful marker of a love of nature and a gift for dowsing

A loop of sensitivity signals a sixth sense

Music loops are common on musicians and dancers as they reveal a strong responsiveness to rhythm

Whorls of isolation are rare and show an intensely private person who needs time alone

Random markings like crosses, stars and circles are of minor importance and will come and go over time

Obscure markings always relate to the part of the hand they are found on

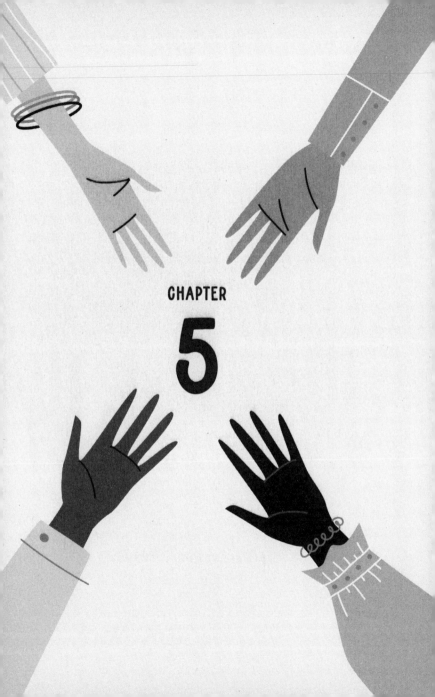

CHAPTER

5

PRACTISING ON REAL HANDS

IVY'S HAND

Now it's time to put all we've learned into practice. The hands shown on the next pages are the hands of Ivy, a 34-year-old, unmarried hypnotherapist. Fingerprints have also been highlighted to aid identification. Try and see what you can discover from Ivy's hands before continuing to read my observations and conclusions. An important thing to note before you begin is that Ivy's dominant hand is her right.

The first thing to note is that the skin quality is silky. This indicates a highly sensitive individual (she hates noise and pollution). Ivy needs a healthy diet and low-stress lifestyle. Next, look at the palm shape. The square palm and long fingers make this an air element hand. Ivy is likely to be tall and thin; she inhabits the world of ideas, and she values her independence. She's a quirky non-conformist.

The Venus mount is slightly enlarged on the active palm. This suggests her energy levels are high and indicates passion for life.

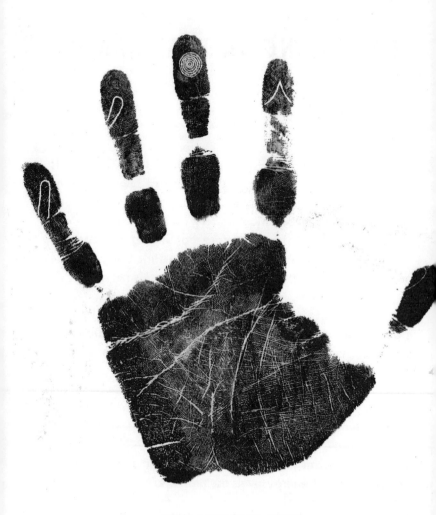

IVY'S LEFT HAND PRINT

Extra information:
- stiff thumb
- large Venus mount
- short Jupiter finger
- silk skin

IVY'S RIGHT HAND PRINT

IVY'S FINGERS

Now look at the fingers. The Mercury finger on the active palm is slightly bent, showing a gift for diplomacy and the capacity to bend the truth. As for the phalanges, the lower and higher levels are well developed, whereas all middle phalanges are small. The large lower sections show a high degree of sensuality. The large higher phalanges reveal a fascination with philosophy, ideals and abstract concepts. The weak middle phalanges show a lack of organization and perhaps some slowness to put plans into action.

The Jupiter fingers on both hands are short, with a tented arch on the passive hand and an ulnar loop on the active hand. Ivy has a lot of self-doubt and can at times feel inadequate. Her sense of personal power and responsibility may not have been reinforced in childhood, and for this reason she needs to avoid self-neglect. The tented arch on the passive palm indicates that Ivy is idealistic and excitable; she may even be overly dramatic on occasion.

The Saturn digit has an ulnar loop on the active hand and a whorl on the passive. This indicates Ivy is a latent rebel who is obsessed with freedom – a whorl on this digit is common on those who marry late or never.

The Apollo digit is long on both hands with a whorl on the active. This shows that Ivy loves attention and needs a form of self-expression, such as painting or photography. The whorl suggests a sharp dress sense and a gift for design, colour and style.

The Mercury digits are particularly long, showing eloquence and wit, and the ability to use language effectively.

The thumbs are stiff. The stiffness reveals that Ivy pushes herself hard to achieve goals and the whorl shows that in her professional life, she's a self-starter and is quite original in her approach.

IVY'S LINES
Moving on to the lines, and starting with the life line, there's a good, wide-sweeping life line on the active hand, but on the passive palm, the bottom section is missing. In Ivy's outer life (represented by her active hand), she's energetic and grounded, with good, regular habits and lifestyle. However, in her home life (portrayed by her passive hand), she's insecure and ungrounded. As a child, stable family structures were not reinforced.

The heart line has a "barbed wire" quality. Ivy can't put her whole heart into relationships, and she can over-intellectualize her feelings. As a result, her emotions are complex and muddled. As her heart line ends under her Jupiter finger, she's idealistic but not as empathetic as she could be.

The head line is extremely long and straight on both palms. Ivy has an unsentimental, analytical nature, and is highly intelligent. She thinks rationally, and is philosophical, always speculating on possibilities.

The fate line is present only in fragments on the passive hand, and curves up from the Lunar mount on the active palm. Ivy is uncertain about who she is in her personal life, and can't commit to relationships. However, at work she finds fulfilment and is clear about her aims. For example, she loves to work with people. Her work and lifestyle may well be vastly different from her family's wishes. This is one of many signs (as well as short Jupiter fingers, missing base of life line, poor-quality heart line) indicating that Ivy's early life might have been problematic.

Of the minor lines, the most obvious are the passion lines on both palms revealing that Ivy has a highly erotic sensibility. Re-examine the prints, make sure you understand each point now I have explained it fully and see if you can make any further observations of your own.

DAVID'S HAND

Now you're on your own! Take a deep breath and calm your mind. It's time for you to examine a palm by yourself and to answer some questions based on your newly acquired expertise. Hopefully, you'll be delighted to discover just how much you can find out about David from a study of his active palm. If in doubt, just refer back to the book's learning points, or to the relevant chapter, to refresh your memory. I'll offer my answers on page 106, and then reveal who David is to see if either of our observations match with the man in question.

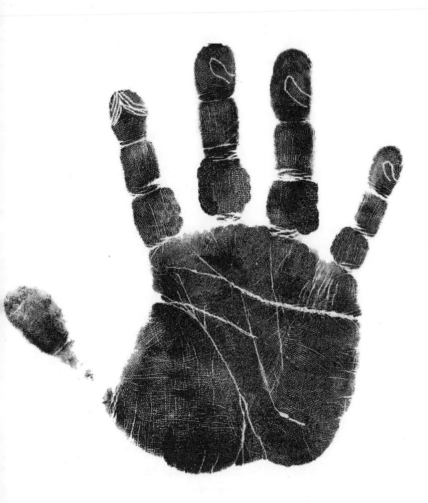

DAVID'S HAND PRINT

QUESTIONS TO CONSIDER

1. What hand shape is this? Is this a tall, freedom loving, cerebral person? What body type are they likely to have?

2. The skin texture is grainy – what does this combination of elemental hand shape and skin texture create when put together? Would this person make a natural computer programmer?

3. David has a large Venus mount. Would he be lethargic and lack energy, or energetic and bursting with spirit?

4. Do any levels of the phalanges stand out as extra large or small?

5. What does the print of the thumb tell you? Does it show a consistent attitude to endeavour and single-minded use of will power?

6. Is the Jupiter finger of normal length? If not, what can you say about it? What does the print on the Jupiter digit tell you? Is he someone hypersensitive to the needs of others and a people pleaser?

7. Look at the Saturn finger – is David likely to be conventional in his attitude to authority?

8. Is the Apollo digit long or short? What does this mean?

9. Looking at the life line, is David an insecure, rootless person?

10. Now let's examine the heart line. Is he cold-hearted or anti-social? What's his emotional nature?

11. Now examine the head line. Is David an introverted, inward-looking dreamer? Can you describe the way he thinks?

12. Look at the fate line next. Could he be employed in a secure, pension-paying job? Or would he choose a more social, artistic and personal career path?

13. The minor lines should be examined at this point — there are some little lines reaching upward from the top of the life line, an Apollo line, and a travel line on this palm. What do they mean?

14. Can you provide a brief summing up of David's character?

If you answer each question as completely as you can, milking each point for the maximum information, you'll have plenty to go on.

ANSWERS ABOUT DAVID'S HANDS

Here are the answer's to the questions above. See if you were right and caught all the details.

QUESTION 1
This is an earth hand (square palm, short fingers), indicating that David is not a cerebral person (air type). Instead, earth types are pragmatic, grounded, earthy personalities who are focused on home, family and security. David's body type will be short and stocky.

QUESTION 2
No, this is not the hand of a computer programmer. The grainy skin and earth palm make for an action-orientated, physical type who is always busy and physically doing stuff; David will not sit around staring at a computer.

QUESTION 3
A large, full Venus mount is common on earth hands and gives a tremendous amount of energy and passion for life. Combined with the physicality of the earth hand shape and the dynamism of the grainy skin, this shows David is a person of great vitality.

QUESTION 4
The lower phalanges are definitely on the large side. This will make David a sensual, pleasure-seeking type, who prioritizes food and physical pleasures. Such temptations may mean he'll have to watch his weight. His middle and higher phalanges are normal.

QUESTION 5

The thumb print is a composite loop. This gives a duality and hesitancy in making decisions about how to push forward in life. It can create doubt and confusion over how to go about getting what he wants.

QUESTION 6

The Jupiter digit is short. This indicates David has a slight inferiority complex and may suffer with self-doubt. He may try to compensate for this by trying to impress others too much. The print on Jupiter is a tented arch. This isn't the sign of a people pleaser (that would be indicated by a radial loop). The tented arch is a sign of an intense, restless personality who's got a strong sense of drama.

QUESTION 7

The Saturn digit is short, so David is going to be unconventional, and is likely to defy authority in some way. This makes for an unusual personality in that he is security seeking and pragmatic (earth hand) but deeply unconventional. The print on this finger is an ulnar loop, which can be ignored.

QUESTION 8

The Apollo finger is long, so David will need an outlet to show off his talents in some way. He might (given that he has an earth palm with a large Venus mount) do a physical sport or craft something to express his talents.

QUESTION 9

The life line is of good quality and complete, so David is grounded, secure and stable. He has abundant energy, can support himself, hold his ground and keep going when things get difficult. He can provide a stable and fixed life for himself and his family.

QUESTION 10

David has a long, clear upturning heart line with a straight branch at the end. This indicates a passionate, romantic and expressive gamut of emotions with a full spectrum of feelings and responses. He will connect emotionally to lots of people. The straight branch at the end shows a part of him that loves reaching out in a caring way toward others.

QUESTION 11

This short, clear, straight head line is the opposite of the introverted dreamer. He is very pragmatic and level-headed. Given that he's an earth person with lots of drive, he's going to be a non-reflective soul who enacts all his ideas. David tends to not look at life philosophically, but instead puts all his energy into getting stuff done. He is likely to be very dynamic, living very much in the real world. He is guilty of never seeing things from a bigger perspective.

QUESTION 12

The fate line beginning in the Lunar mount is a sign that David has chosen a career and lifestyle that is based on social connections and sense of personal fulfilment. He has not sought a secure, stable profession. If we add in the short Saturn finger, we've got a person who's stable, security conscious, but deeply alternative in his life direction.

QUESTION 13

The small lines on the top of the life line are effort lines, which denote an ambitious person. There is a clear, long Apollo line present, which shows David feels fulfilled and content – he will love his own company and will be involved in a practice or art that gives him a sense of losing himself. The travel line at the base of the life line shows a love of travel and a sense of adventure.

QUESTION 14

So, to sum up David's character, we have a person full of contradictions. He is a solid, down-to-earth person with a pragmatic attitude to life who values tradition, family and home. He has a lively, energetic nature; his grainy skin and Venus mount tells us he's never one to sit around for long. However, there are aspects of his personality that run opposite to his deeper instincts. He has a tented arch print on his Jupiter finger, which is a sign of intensity and someone that seeks drama. He also has a short Saturn finger, which makes him unconventional, and his fate line indicates he has chosen a fulfilling life path that's far from the conventions of his background. We can also see a composite loop print on David's thumb, which shows he has a vacillating attitude when making life decisions. The Jupiter digit is short, so he's got a sense of never feeling up to the mark and his long Apollo finger gives a sense of wanting to display or show off some talent or ability.

Looking at the phalanges, his large lower phalanges give a sensual love of food and pleasure. Moving onto the lines, his strong life line suggests stability and security, though the travel line will need movement and adventure in his life. The short head line is the sign (as if we needed any more) that he is an active, dynamic doer and someone that puts all his ideas and skills into practice. This is not a philosopher by any stretch of the imagination. The heart line indicates a passionate, expressive, romantic soul who pours his heart into life, with a sense of compassion for others. The fate line shows us he won't be a postman or a council worker. He's obviously found contentment and loves what he does, given his Apollo line's length and his aspiration lines (fine lines running upward near the top of the life line) mean he'll go far and push himself hard. However, with the short Jupiter and composite print on this thumb, he'll avoid too much responsibility and will apply himself in a sort of stop–go manner, with lots of change and variety.

SO HOW DID YOU DO?

David is a grounded, pragmatic, highly energetic person with an alternative lifestyle who is nonetheless ambitious. He is a chef, who works around the country from a mobile pop-up restaurant that promotes alternative living, vegetarianism and conservation. This gives him the alternative lifestyle he wants (short Saturn finger) along with travel and adventure (travel line) and indulges his large lower phalanges phalanges as he loves fresh, high-quality food.

David takes his family on most of his work outings and they all pitch in and help. He began with a small van but now operates out of a large set of mobile structures that provide a colourful restaurant setting and he has become very affluent, supporting his family comfortably (good life line, effort lines). He works in various fairs, festivals and events and has become something of a minor celebrity, appearing on local TV and in various magazines – this gives his long Apollo finger an outlet.

He has had lots of opportunities to push his business to a higher level but lacks the confidence and doesn't want too much responsibility (short Jupiter finger) and is ambivalent about committing himself to one single activity (composite on thumb) so he is always open to trying out different options and working commitments.

He is a passionate vegetarian and has fought his local authority to make this the norm in some local schools (short Saturn finger). He started a free kitchen for the homeless (compassionate extra section to heart line) and is a very generous soul. He never stops working, travelling and doing stuff. He speaks three languages, has learned to build and design his own mobile structures and is a qualified horseman. He rarely reflects on life but believes in doing and acting with no time for long discussion (short head line).

He has a smallholding where he grows herbs and exotic vegetables and plants and where he loses himself for hours, getting close to nature (Apollo line). David would definitely say he is a contented soul.

So how did you do? Of course, you weren't expected to know *how* David would live out the patterns in his palm, but hopefully, you could pick out some of the deeper qualities and contradictions of his personality (earthy, dynamic, passionate, intense, rebellious, kind, alternative lifestyle, etc). Of course, this was only a thumbnail sketch of the right palm. We would have had more work to do if we examined the left as well.

FINAL THOUGHTS

As you grow into a serious palm reader, you may well find you can only pick out a few things in a palm at first — maybe the shape and skin, and perhaps an unusual (non-ulnar) print. This might only give you ten minutes' worth of things to say to a person, but that is nonetheless a great start.

You can always proceed by gently asking some questions to confirm your observations. For example, if you think a person has silky skin, ask them, "Would you consider yourself extremely sensitive?" Or if you have identified a fire hand with grainy skin, you could ask them, "Do you find you are always restless and on the go?"

Look at every palm on every person you can. Each hand has a lesson in it for you. Proceeding in this manner will give you wonderful experience and feedback and will build your confidence as you grow as a palmist. You will then become a great visionary into the soul and inner workings of others. May the journey never end!

QUICK REFERENCE LIST

Active hand: the dominant hand, representing the outward, adult expressed aspects of the personality

Air palm: large, square palm with long fingers, representing a person who is high-minded, lofty and idea-orientated

Apollo finger: the ring finger shows the drive for self-expression, creativity and the need to be liked, admired and to be on the public stage in some way

Apollo line: a fine line running under the apollo finger and beneath the heart line, signifying an inner retreat, a sense of loving one's own company and a sense of contentment

Apollo mount: found directly below the Apollo finger, lines found here are connected to cultural interests, self-aggrandizement and self-expression

Bars: an obstacle that blocks one's path in the short term

Coarse skin: hard, rough skin that shows only a few deep lines on a palm print. This means the person is outdoorsy, tough and hardy

Composite loop: formed by two loops facing in opposite directions, the composite loop shows someone with the ability to see both sides of any situation, patterns of doubt and uncertainty, unable to see things in black and white

Crosses: these show opposing drives in life and a need to make a decision

Duplicates: a doubled line shows two levels of experience of a line's qualities and energy

Earth palm: square and short fingered, signifying a down-to-earth, practical and non-academic person

Effort lines: fine lines running upward off the life line, revealing someone who is ambitious and yearns to climb higher in life

Fate line: running vertically down the centre of the palm, the fate line shows the person's sense of character, sense of direction and sense of self-awareness

Fire palm: rectangular palm with short fingers, revealing a hot-blooded, dynamic and goal-orientated personality

Girdle of Venus: fine horizontal lines above the heart line showing the need for higher experience and escape

Grainy skin: shows firm, hard skin ridges with strong, red lines like cuts on a palm print. This means the person is good at sports, busy, active and has quick physical responses

Head line: begins near the top of the life line and runs across the middle of the palm, showing the extent of mental focus and clarity

Health line: a single line, or series of scratchy lines, running vertically from the base of the palm toward the Mercury mount, showing the condition of the vagus nerve and the person's capacity for mental calm and inspiration

Heart line: horizontal line under the four fingers, representing the person's abilty to emote and express feelings

Inner Mars mount: found just above the thumb, when a line begins here it shows mental or physical toughness

Intuition line: a bow-shaped line running up the ulnar side of the palm below the Mercury finger, showing a connection to the intuitive subconscious

Islands: chain links on broken lines that show signs of stress and difficulty

Jupiter finger: the index finger – the most important as it shows self-reflection, ego, sense of self and personal power

Jupiter mount: found directly below the Jupiter finger; if a line crosses here the person may be battling with issues of ambition, personal power, control or authority

Life line: this line curls around the thumb ball and shows the person's extent of security, fixity of nature and stability of character

Lunar mount: at the base of the ulnar side of the palm, revealing our collective subconscious, moods and dreams

Mars line: short line above the thumb and within the life line, revealing the person's competitive and sporty streak

Mercury finger: the little finger shows the quality of signal, social, and sexual communication

Mercury mount: found directly below the Mercury finger, lines here relate to commerce, communication, eloquence, deception, sexual sophistication and wit

Outer Mars mount: found on the outer edge of the ulnar side in the middle, and when it swells out it indicates a pushy, enthusiastic character

Paper skin: papery, dry skin that shows tightly grained, fine skin ridges with long, scratchy lines on a palm print. This means the person is responsive to visual and verbal stimuli

Passion line: angular line connecting the heart line to the base of the Mercury mount, revealing a need for passion and eroticism in their sex life

Passive hand: the non-dominant hand, representing the inner, childhood, latent aspects of personality

Phalanges: each finger is separated into the higher, middle and lower phalanges

Plain of Mars: never raised and therefore simply an area of the palm instead of a mount

Pluto mount: found at the base of the radial side, this mount is only significant when a line crosses it

Radial loop: the same pattern as the ulnar loop but facing the opposite direction, flowing away from the thumb rather than toward it; it signifies someone who is hyper-responsive, eager to please, defensive and vulnerable to losing their sense of self in other's need

Radial side: when the palm is split in half, the radial side is the side with the thumb

Ring of Solomon: a faint line around the base of the Jupiter finger, symbolizing the ability to see into others

Saturn finger: the middle finger; the digit of normality, rules, work, conventions, institutions and family

Saturn mount: found directly below the Saturn finger, if a line crosses here the person may be having issues with restrictions, rules and life committments

Silk skin: soft skin that shows barely visible ridges and lots of fine lines on a palm print. This means the person is extremely sensitive and highly aware of atmospheres, tastes and energies

Simian line: an unusual bonding of head and heart lines, giving a fixed, intense, highly focused and repressed personality

Simple arch: formed from an almost flat chevron formation of lines piled on top of one another, the simple arch shows someone highly loyal, repressive, hard-working and security-conscious

Teacher's square: a faint square on the Jupiter mount, showing good management, organising and teaching abilities

Tented arch: forming a sharp spike pointing skyward, the tented arch shows someone who is excitable, intense, dramatic and needs excitement and rest

Travel lines: branches at the base of the life line showing a drive for adventure and travel

Ulnar loop: the most common pattern, the ulnar loop is a wave shape and indicates a "go with the flow" mentality.

Ulnar side: when the palm is split in half, the ulnar side is the furthest from the thumb

Water palm: narrow rectangular palm with long fingers, representing someone who is adaptable and people-orientated

Whorl: formed of a series of ever-decreasing circles or a spiral formation, the whorl is a marker of independence, originality, love of solitude and the ability to work alone

Venus mount: the large, fleshy mount at the base of the thumb showing whether the person is energetic or not

Via lascivia: a curved line at the base of the palm on the Lunar mount, indicating an obsession with health, allergies and a likely over-responsive immune system

FURTHER READING

Beaven, Don & Brooks, Stafford Eric, *Colour Atlas of The Nail in Clinical Diagnosis*, Mosby, 1984

Benham, W, *The Laws of Scientific Hand Reading*, 1900, reprinted as *The Benham Book of Palmistry*, Newcastle, 1988

Brandon-Jones, D, *Your Palm: Barometer of Health*, Rider, 1985

Clifford, F, *Palmistry 4 Today*, Flare Books, 2010

Clifford, F, *Dermatoglyphics in Medical Disorders*, Springer, 1976

Fincham, J, *The Spellbinding Power of Palmistry*, Green Magic, 2009

Fitzherbert, A, *Hand Psychology*, Avery Publishing Group, 1989

Fitzherbert, A & Altman, N, *Palmistry: Your Career in Your Hands*, Aquarian, 1989

Gettings, F, *The Book of the Hand*, Hamlyn, 1965

Gettings, F, *The Book of Palmistry*, Tribune Books, 1974, reprinted as *Palmistry*, Chancellor Press, 1993

Hutchinson, B, *Your Life in Your Hands*, Sphere, 1967

Jaquin, N, *The Hand Speaks*, London, 1942

Manning, J T, *The Finger Book*, Faber and Faber, 2009

Scheimann, E & Altman, N, *Medical Palmistry*, Aquarian, 1989

Wolff, C, *The Hand in Psychological Diagnosis*, Methuen, 1951

Websites: www.johnnyfincham.com and www.handanalysis.co.uk

ACKNOWLEDGEMENTS

With grateful thanks to my many students and clients over the years who have taught me so much. Thanks also to Jo Richardson and Jai-Jai for all-round loveliness.

INDEX